Macdonald Insiders

Hotel

Carol Wright

Macdonald Educational

Editor Julia Kirk
Design Robert Wheeler
Production Philip Hughes
Picture Research Jenny Golden

Macdonald Educational Ltd
Holywell House
Worship Street
London EC2A 2EN

Printed by New Interlitho,
Milan, Italy

First published 1978

ISBN 0 356 05586 8

Hotel

Contents

The layout of a modern hotel

Hotels through the ages

Hotels come in all shapes, sizes and characters: modern skyscrapers with the latest furnishings and fittings, centuries-old country inns, converted manor houses, castles, monasteries or convents. In India they can be former maharajahs' palaces, in Portugal, old fortresses. Hotels can be grand, with a member of staff for every guest, or they can be homely and small and run by a husband and wife team.

Hotels can be traced back centuries before Christ was born in a stable because of an early overbooking problem at Bethlehem's inn. The Romans had an efficient network of posting houses on the roads throughout their empire.

Inns until after the middle ages had a poor reputation and it was only pilgrims who travelled for pleasure rather than necessity. Kings stayed with nobles, but for the ordinary traveller at an inn, there was no privacy. A traveller ate his food he carried with him in a communal room; mattresses were laid out in dormitories; beds, if available, were shared. The Great Bed of Ware, built for an inn, slept sixty-eight people 'spoon' fashion – head to toe. There was also the problem of lice and bed-bugs. Parson Woodford in 1783 stayed at the *Belle Sauvage*, a famous London inn 'and was bit terribly by bugs'.

'Lodging and clean sheets 3s; dirty sheets 1s.' ran an inn tariff in New York in 1798. But it was in America where the hotel as we know it was invented. The Tremont Hotel was opened in Boston in 1829 with 170 rooms. It was the first hotel to print menus and give free soap – a custom still not widely practised. Other innovations in the hotel were eight water closets, eight 'bathing rooms' in the basement and buzzers for the first room service.

Cesar Ritz, in Europe, encouraged private bathrooms and created a home-from-home for the rich. Statler in America built the first commercial hotel for the travelling salesman with bathrooms for every room, free morning paper, and rooms wired for radio. Conrad Hilton produced the businessman's luxury hotel with high standards of plumbing world-wide.

The motel, a low-level hotel for motorists on tour, with parking space alongside rooms, was first seen in 1924. It really developed after World War II when the Holiday Inn and Howard Johnson chains in the United States produced reliable standard rooms. In 1903 the Hertfordshire Public House Trust Company was formed to restore old coaching inns which had declined with the arrival of railways. The Wagon and Horse at St Albans was the first of these Trust Houses, but is now only one of eight hundred international properties owned by the company.

Some facts and figures

A typical large city hotel can sleep 1500 people in 826 bedrooms; 104 single, 654 twin-bedded and 68 double-bedded.

To service this, 700 staff are needed, including some part-time banqueting staff. For them 934 uniforms are made.

To furnish such a hotel, the shopping list includes 31,000 square metres of carpet and 31,000 square metres of underlay, 18,000 metres of curtaining and 1,608 metres of net curtain.

In the rooms go 9,322 coat hangers, 1,026 pictures, 4,470 ashtrays, 1,994 waste paper baskets.

To keep guests in clean bedlinen, the hotel must keep stocks of 5,560 blankets, 10,824 sheets, 11,210 pillow cases, 3,550 pillows, 1,725 bedspreads, 10,836 towels and 3,000 bath mats.

Each week the hotel must launder 50,000 pieces of linen.

In the restaurants and for room service, further items are needed in bulk:
18,600 pieces of cutlery, 10,865 pieces of glass ware, 16,715 pieces of china, 2,956 jugs, 993 teapots and 729 coffee pots.

▼ This is the Old Swan Hotel at Lavenham. It is typical of old coaching inns and would originally have had stables for horses.

Working in a hotel

A hotel, they say, is only as good as its staff. Dr Johnson said 'there is nothing which has yet been contrived by man by which so much happiness is produced as by a good tavern or inn'. Today when hotel buildings are often identical in comfort and facilities, the courtesy and efficiency of the staff are vital for success.

In some ways, the organization of a hotel is like that of a great house. In fact, many famous hotels were started by ex-servants of noblemen. During the French Revolution many aristocrats were executed and their lands confiscated. Their out-of-work servants started hotels. That was when the word was first used. 'Hotel' also meant in French, a mansion or large house.

In England, William Claridge, an ex-servant, set up a hotel at 49 Brook Street in London in the mid-nineteenth century at the request of King George IV who wanted somewhere to meet his friends without fuss. Claridges today maintains a principle of protecting aristocratic clientele and other famous guests from unwanted publicity.

Certain clothing ideas from the households of noble families also live on in hotels. The manager in some of the more traditional, old-fashioned hotels may wear a frock coat and striped trousers as correct as any *Upstairs, Downstairs* butler. Page boys have buttoned uniforms with white gloves tucked under epaulettes, and carry messages and run errands in the smarter hotels. The porter may have a buttoned uniform and the doorman's top hat and cape coat recall the uniform

of the coachman of times gone by.

Whatever the size of a hotel, team-work is vital. If the maid does not finish her room on time, the arriving guest may go to another hotel. Bad service brings complaints and a bad reputation for the hotel. Hotels are, after all, businesses dealing with people, and all nationalities and customs come together in hotels. In some prestige hotels this can be exciting and provide the fun of seeing pop stars, kings, bishops, dukes and duchesses, tycoons and important people at close quarters.

But hotels cannot exist on these customers alone. Many now take big tour groups who have little time and money to spare and who want fast service. It's hard work checking tourists in by the dozen, making sure that their luggage is sorted out and that their rooms are recleaned for another group the next day. Businessmen also want quick service, messages relayed correctly, drinks and meals brought to their room, shirts cleaned in a day and a fast check out.

Airline crews may want meals and service in the middle of the night. In motels everyone clamours to leave immediately after breakfast. And in seaside and resort areas, there may be old, lonely people who live in a hotel and come to regard the staff as their only family. Hotels are hard work – they never close. It is a twenty-four hour job for the staff, who see life and death, crime and passion, and who must be equally polite and understanding to both bad-tempered or appreciative guests.

Preparing a guest's room

Twenty years ago Conrad Hilton wrote in his autobiography, 'Any new hotel of the future should include the following: TV, portable libraries, sun lamps, portable beauty parlours, small freezers for ice cubes in each room, automatic telephones that record all calls, improved air conditioning and ventilation equipment'. Not all these things have yet arrived. The era of the disposable bedsheet is on its way, and many hotels have tea and coffee makers, mini-fridge bars and televisions in each room, all of which have to be cleaned and checked by the maid.

Once maids carried heavy trays, bowls of hot water for guests to wash in, coal for their fires, filled hot water bottles and set out candles at night. But nowadays the typical check list for smaller items is even more daunting.

Breakfast order forms and 'do not disturb notices' must be hung on door knobs, coat hangers placed in wardrobes and laundry and dry cleaning lists in drawers. Cards advertising hotel and tour services must be set out and a stationery folder must be filled with notepaper, envelopes and a pen. Many hotels provide telephone directories and even bibles. Ashtrays and matches are set out and the room finished with a spray from an air freshener.

Conrad Hilton was only one of many individuals who have tried to bring a personal touch to the decoration of hotels. This has resulted in many antiquated and out of date hotels being modernized and made more friendly and welcoming for the guest.

An eye for detail and good colour sense are important in housekeeping for hotels. Senior housekeepers say red is the most practical colour and that blue and green soon look shabby. Everyone concerned with preparing a hotel room needs to know how to make it look attractive and clean. But it is the chambermaid who can ensure that the finer touches are carried out: neat hospital bed corners, pillows the right way up and neatly squared and curtains pulled evenly.

Good housekeepers keep a note of the needs of regular and VIP guests and can provide many additional comforts such as bed boards, soft or hard pillows, baby bottle warmers, playpens and extra lights and beds as required. They take pride in arranging flowers or a bowl of fruit in a room to provide an extra special welcome for a VIP.

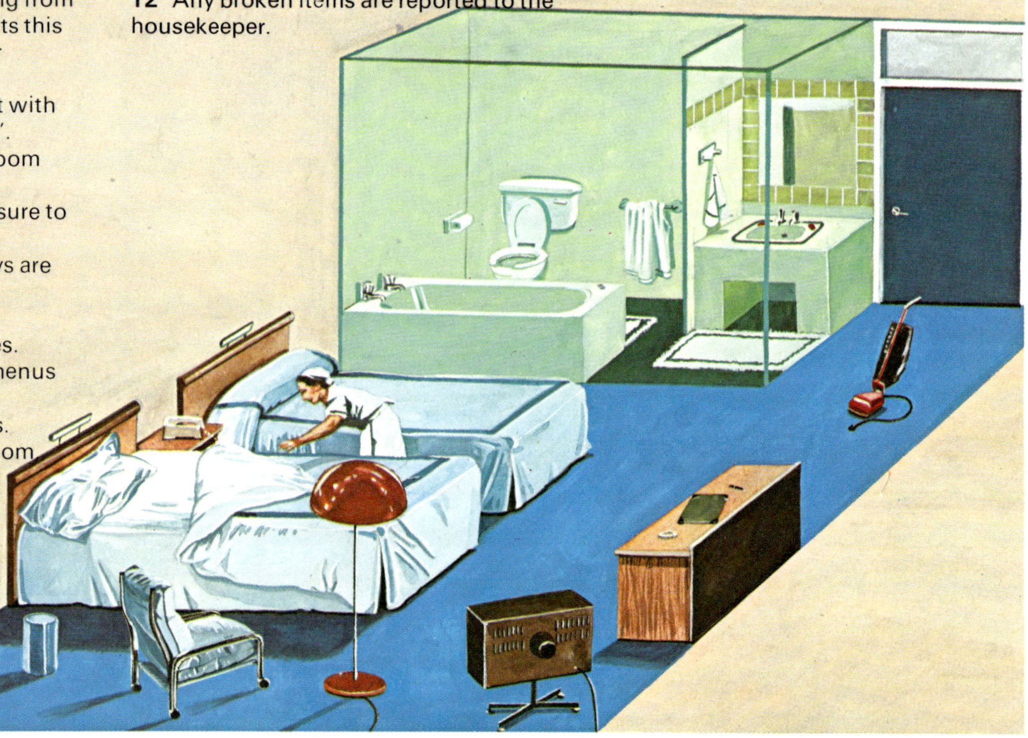

Preparing a bedroom

Each room must be thoroughly cleaned before it is ready for occupation. The chambermaid has a list of duties:

1 She checks for property left behind by guests. She checks anything missing from the room taken by guests and reports this by telephone to the housekeeper or reception.

2 She strips the bed and remakes it with clean linen, using 'hospital corners'.

3 Windows are opened to air the room if necessary.

4 She hoovers the carpet, making sure to hoover under the bed.

5 Waste paper baskets and ashtrays are emptied and cleaned if necessary.

6 She polishes or cleans all room surfaces, particularly dressing tables.

7 She replaces hotel notices and menus on dressing table, putting out fresh notepaper, pads, pens and matches.

8 Towels are removed from bathroom, glasses are cleaned or changed.

9 She cleans the bathroom and its floor, paying special attention to the toilet.

10 She replaces fresh towels, adds new soap and tissues if necessary.

11 She checks that room and bathroom lights work.

12 Any broken items are reported to the housekeeper.

► Room service is available in most large hotels. Guests can order their breakfast by telephone. Many hotels now have printed order forms which the guest fills out and hangs on the outside of his door before he goes to sleep.

▲ The maid here is putting a final touch to a room. She has already cleaned thoroughly and has made up the bed. The floor housekeeper is telephoning reception to tell them the room is ready, has been checked, and can be let.

◄ Chambermaids are provided with trolleys, which are stocked with all the equipment and linen needed for the rooms.

▲ The floor housekeeper is filling a small refrigerator bar which is in a guest's bedroom. The guest helps himself and is billed for what he drinks.

Housekeepers

The team in charge of making sure the hotel looks comfortable and tidy is the housekeeping department. Some hotels have over a thousand rooms to be cleaned every day to say nothing of public rooms, ballrooms, and lengthy corridors. As well as making sure everything looks attractive, is in its place and in good working order, housekeeping staff must check lost property, keep an eye on guests' movements, assist in security and fire procedures and get rooms ready for new arrivals on time.

Head housekeeper

The housekeeper controls all the guest accommodation, its cleaning and servicing. Her work largely consists of supervising the work of her staff and checking that it is up to standard. She has an annual budget and is entrusted to spend it wisely to make the hotel look its best.

She must decide when to replace or repair curtains, carpets, lamp shades or pillows and try to keep cleaning costs down. Dry cleaning of bedspreads alone runs to several thousands of pounds a year in a large hotel. She must also check furnishings and supplies and is sometimes asked by manufacturers to try out new cleaning products and fabrics.

The housekeeper is responsible for hiring and training the maids, seamstresses, linen porters and valets under her control. She reports on their progress and recommends them for promotion if she feels they deserve it.

The housekeeper's day starts by checking in the maids and giving them work schedules and keys. During the morning she compiles weekly time sheets and overtime sheets and meets with other department heads for discussions. She may talk about the annual spring cleaning needed, look at advance booking numbers, and check on special VIP arrangements. She makes spot checks on her staff and the cleanliness of the rooms. She will also be concerned with security checks on rooms and reports of thefts.

In appearance, like her staff, she must dress neatly. Housekeepers often live in the hotel but usually work a 9-5 day. There is a fair amount of paper work to do, ordering supplies, checking reports, making reports for the manager on lost property, damage to rooms and security. Complaints and crises involving the rooms will also involve her attention.

The housekeeper supervises the linen room and occasionally checks linen for replacement. Checks are also kept on bath towels and wash cloths, which tend to disappear rapidly. Each day the housekeeper must check corridors and public areas to ensure these have been properly cleaned. She also checks that carpets are not frayed or holed and liable to cause an accident.

Deputy housekeeper

Larger hotels may have a deputy housekeeper whose job is to assist the housekeeper. The deputy must take over the housekeeper's job in the event of illness or absence and in general carry out her instructions and look after staff.

Floor housekeeper

Big hotels also have floor housekeepers. As their name suggests, each is in charge of one floor of the hotel. They are responsible for the work of the maids on their floor and the maintenance of that floor's appearance as well as supervising its linen, security, and valeting. They will also look after such items as hairdriers or irons that are loaned to guests on request. This job is a step towards becoming a housekeeper.

► The works manager discusses the redecoration and annual cleaning of some bedrooms with the maids.

Valet

The valet is responsible for collecting dry cleaning and personal laundry at the request of guests. He must make sure that it is cleaned and pressed, whether inside or outside the hotel, and make any minor repairs as necessary. He must then return it to the guest's room with the bill copy. Though most hotels now provide machines or polishing cloths for shoe cleaning, in some hotels the valet will clean shoes left outside doors overnight.

Room maid

The room maid's job varies in the hours worked and a maid can either work part-time or she may be a student – one way of finding out if you like hotel life. Some maids live in, others are local residents. Evening maids, who turn down bed covers, draw curtains, and tidy the rooms for the night, are part-time.

Maids are responsible to the floor or general housekeeper depending on the hotel's size. They check in and out each day with their immediate superior. On arrival they are given an allocation of rooms and keys which must be returned after work. The number of rooms one maid will have to clean varies, but the average is 9-15 each. The maids have special service rooms on each floor where they keep their belongings and trolleys, and change into their uniform.

Most hotels provide uniforms or overalls and expect maids to be tidy with a minimum of makeup and jewellery and hair tied back neatly. Each maid has a trolley with bags for dirty linen and rubbish, shelves for cleaning materials, mops, notepaper, tissues, soaps, matches and other items they have to replace in the guests' rooms.

The maid's daily duty starts by checking any unused rooms and dusting as needed. Honouring 'do not disturb' notices on the doors of still sleeping guests, she cleans vacated rooms, tidying guests' belongings if still occupied. Each hotel has its own system of cleaning and each maid is taught by other senior maids or by the housekeeper. For example, Holiday Inns have done work studies on how long certain jobs take. To make one of their double beds takes 7-8 minutes on average, and to clean a whole room from start to finish is 30 minutes.

Instructions to maids may include sending soiled linen down a chute, dusting from the top downwards before hoovering, and always to pay special attention to toilets. Check lists and work plans may be provided. The maid's work is inspected by her superiors and during training she will receive briefings on security, told how to knock and enter a room, how to greet guests, what to do in case of fire, theft or illness.

The hours of work will be roughly eight hours a day with meal breaks. Late morning will be the busiest when guests have left and before new arrivals come in.

House porter

Working under the direction of the housekeeper, the house porter copes with heavy work, bringing linen on request from the linen room to floors where needed. If no laundry chutes are installed, he carries soiled linen to the linen room.

He helps move service food trays from corridors, tidies the lift areas, cleans vending machines in the corridors, moves beds if requested, takes up carpets and shifts furniture as requested by the housekeeper.

Head linen keeper

This person looks after all the hotel linen – sheets, pillowcases and towels. He or she must supervise the linen staff in the counting of dirty linen, check in clean linen from the laundry and control the linen issued to maids and other staff. Repairs to uniforms and stock taking are other duties.

Linen porter

The linen porters help the head linen keeper in counting all items going in and out of the hotel, loading and unloading delivery vans from the laundry and cleaning the linen room.

▶ The head housekeeper personally supervises the finishing touches to a room to be occupied by a VIP. Flowers, fruit, and chocolates are among the extras offered.

The lobby

The lobby or entrance area of a hotel is its heart and busiest place. People come and go continually, luggage piles up, the doorman summons taxis, cars and tour buses arrive full of new guests for the hotel, or ready to take away those leaving. People stand around waiting to meet friends, or call them from the bank of house telephones. Travel-weary guests, some in colourful national dress, stand waiting to check in; conference delegates with huge name badges talk loudly, waiting to be shown up to their special conference suite.

Cesar Ritz, the founder of the great Ritz hotels, did not like lounges and lobbies; he felt they encouraged too many loiterers. He seems to have been proved right on this point, since some hotels have such stunning and unusual lobbies that people may visit the hotel just to stand and stare. After all, the lobby is the focal point of the hotel and the part which the guest will first see on arrival. It is therefore important that the lobby creates the right impression of friendliness and welcome for the guest. Individually designed interiors help to give the hotel character.

One of the most famous is in the Hyatt Hotel in Atlanta, Georgia, where room balconies look down over the vast lobby below with its decorative central bars and seating area. The lifts are illuminated cigar-shaped cages, speeding up and down on the inside of the multi-storey lobby – to be seen and see from, if you have a head for heights!

The Oberoi in Colombo has a big square lobby hung with massive batik banners the depth of the building. The London Ritz has a long gallery centred by the famous Palm Court, in which people enjoy sitting, to see other guests and be seen themselves. And many hotels have covered garden-like areas in the lobby with fountains and exotic plants.

Working in the hotel lobby

The lobby is never still. In the middle of the night airline crews or overseas tours may arrive. By the time breakfast is over, the cashier's area is busy with people checking out. Nearby the receptionists are working out the day's guest lists and receiving the first guests of the day; a pattern that will go on with mounting pressure until the evening.

The Head Porter's desk occupies a vantage point in the lobby where he can see everything that goes on. Underporters carry luggage in and out, and in larger hotels, messenger boys in braided and buttoned uniforms go round with boards searching for a guest to deliver a message. By the lifts stand the uniformed liftmen and outside the main door is the doorman signalling for taxis, opening car doors and assisting guests in and out of the hotel.

The manager takes a look round as he arrives; the lobby is, after all, the hotel's shop window and it must look tidy and attractive.

In large hotels services are grouped round the lobby. There may be a hostess at a hospitality desk ready to answer queries and help guests or conference delegates.

Earlier in the day, the flowergirl will open up her kiosk and start rearranging flowers in the lobby and perhaps on the reception desk as well as making up displays for the guests' rooms.

The lobby is where the 'grapevine' of the hotel begins. The staff keep an eye on the guests' movements and by observing them can pass on helpful advice to colleagues. Security starts in the lobby; sometimes there is a security desk near the door where everyone's hand luggage is searched. This has resulted mainly from bomb attacks made by terrorists in hotels.

Receptionists and the hall porter's staff are trained to watch guests discreetly to note any strange behaviour, and watch out for any unattended parcels or bags. They also try and assess guests who might try and leave without paying. Leaving empty cases with the porter and the declaration 'I'll be back soon' is one way this has been done.

Luggage, of course, is always present in any lobby, with porters labelling and checking it in and out and arranging for its dispatch to rooms. Many hotels have a special luggage room, where luggage which has been sent on ahead can be stored until the guest arrives at the hotel and claims it.

As well as the reception area for checking in and the adjacent cashier's office for money transactions, the lobby often contains a book stall, small souvenir shops, a hairdressing salon, a tour operator's desk and hospitality desks.

The lobby will also be specially decorated for Christmas and other festivals. One hotel had a magnificent Easter display complete with live rabbits; the rabbits were, alas, stolen.

In a large lobby or in adjacent lounge areas, morning coffee and afternoon tea may be served. Large city hotels are the best places now for an elegant tea served with small sandwiches and pastries, usually made in the hotel. In some American hotels, a girl will wheel round a portable bar to serve guests sitting in the lobby.

The receptionist's office

The hotel of the future may be so streamlined that a credit card pushed into a slot at a reception desk will automatically check in a guest, rather in the way one can get money from a bank cashpoint. The guest will receive a room allocation and can then collect his key.

Until that happens, the receptionist is the key to the character of a hotel. Whatever the problem, the receptionist, together with the porter's staff, can help to calm the guest and make him or her feel welcome to the hotel.

A receptionist is trained to watch people carefully. This is in the interests of the hotel, since she will become skilful in deciding whether a guest is genuine or whether he is trying to cheat the hotel.

Hotels are often hoodwinked by guests who book themselves in under aristocratic, foreign titles and who then run up vast bills and disappear. Others stay only for one night, giving false addresses, and move on before bills can catch them up. The receptionist must check on names and bookings. People sometimes book single rooms and then try to smuggle friends in late at night – one way of saving money! The receptionist

must report such things to the security officer, who will then take appropriate action.

If a room booked is not yet ready the receptionist must keep the waiting guest happy by suggesting a meal or a drink and showing him to one of the hotel's restaurants or bars. If required, she informs the housekeeping department to make up two twin beds into a double for a double room request. At the same time she may be checking in a group of fifty Japanese tourists, coping with telephone enquiries or handing out keys and mail. Because the receptionist is the person most seen in a hotel she is the one who must deal with the enquiries, the insults and the praise.

Colleagues in the adjacent cashier's office must also be calm and quick-witted. It is their job to make sure that the hotel is not swindled, and they must make up bills accurately and check people out. Usually everyone wants to leave after breakfast when breakfast bills have not arrived and this makes the cashier's job more difficult.

The hall porter's office is constantly busy. He is the source of information for everything that is happening, both inside the hotel and out. He is continually dealing with questions: where is the press reception or conference being held, can he get two tickets for the opera, a car to go to the airport, a children's nurse? Where can Japanese newspapers be bought and can he bring down some luggage urgently?

The hall porter has his staff of luggage porters and messenger boys who run errands and, in a few hotels, will even go out to buy a forgotten toothbrush for a guest!

▲ The porter is responsible for taking guests' luggage as they enter the hotel and for safely delivering it to the right room.

◀ Many big hotels have a tour or theatre ticket agency situated in the lobby. Guests are given information on current events and make bookings for theatres, concerts and films.

▲ While guests sign the register, the receptionist finds their booking card in a rack. This will contain details of the kind of room they have asked for.

Dealing with people

These jobs have much direct contact with the public. Each hotel, according to its size, may have different equipment and space for these jobs but basically the tasks are similar. Most front of house personnel wear a hotel uniform, usually different uniforms for different jobs. In smaller hotels usually plain dark clothing is preferred, and several of these jobs may be dealt with by the same person.

Receptionist

This is the person who presents the welcome of the hotel. She is the first person the guest comes into contact with and so becomes a source of information. The receptionist must be familiar with the whole operation of the hotel from knowing the dish of the day to which rooms have quiet outlooks.

Reception works closely with housekeeping to check when rooms are ready for arriving guests. Tired travellers are never patient about waiting for rooms.

Many hotels now have a light system to tell the receptionist what stage a room has reached. When a maid is cleaning a vacated room, a red and green light show on a panel in reception. When cleaned, the maid switches off the red light and the receptionist knows by the single green light that she can let that room.

Some hotels also have a switch for heating and air conditioning which the receptionist switches on when a guest arrives and off when he leaves. Receptionists work in shifts of about $7\frac{1}{2}$ hours in a team under a supervisor.

Work starts around 7 a.m. for the first shift who must check the previous night's occupancy and the rooms to be vacated. Mail is sorted and placed in guests' pigeon holes. The 'special book' is checked to see which rooms have VIP's, so that fruit or flowers can be placed in the rooms.

Filing and typing up lists of arriving and departing guests is done. As guests arrive, bookings are checked, cash is requested in advance for chance arrivals, imprints are taken of credit cards and passport numbers of foreign guests are noted.

The checking-in process is simplified by a daily rack of cards which give names, booking details and any special needs. While this is being found, the guest fills in a registration card needed by law. The guest is allocated a room and given the key.

More and more hotels now also hand out a key card, which is the guest's authority for signing bills in the hotel and for claiming keys from reception. A small hotel will know its guests by sight, but in large hotels, this cuts down on crime.

The receptionist is responsible for putting keys and messages into pigeon holes under the right room numbers. She will also supervise deposits and withdrawals made from guest safety deposit boxes.

After office hours, the receptionist may also take telephone bookings and will need a knowledge of rates, special discounts and voucher payment systems. She will have an advance bookings chart showing how full the hotel is on each date.

In city hotels, the busiest time is from 4-6 p.m. Guests pour in and the receptionist's work can be eased by allocating rooms in advance to regular and VIP guests. Special parties may also have pre-allocated rooms, with keys put in envelopes which can then be distributed by the group leader.

The receptionist works with the hall porter, telling him a guest's room number so that he can send up the luggage. Sometimes she may conduct a guest to his room.

Cashier

In smaller hotels, the work of cashier and receptionist may be combined. Even in bigger hotels, at busy times each may assist the other. The cashier is responsible for billing the guest and handling money transactions for him.

During his stay she may cash travellers cheques and exchange foreign currency, and a board containing exchange rates is by her desk. Guests may find this more convenient that going to a bank, though hotels usually charge more for this service.

During a guest's stay, bills for various items ordered are sent down by the dining room, laundry, room service, bars and so on. Each day the cashier brings the bill up to date. She knows the credit card limit agreed between hotel and credit card company and if the guest is not known and is spending more than his limit, she sends out standard letters to ask

◀ The cashier keeps each guest's bill up to date, adding in accounts received from bars, restaurants, valet, room service. She also checks credit ratings of unknown guests.

him to pay his account.

She must also know which companies have credit facilities with the hotel. When a guest checks out she must check if he had breakfast on the final morning, if he has drunk anything from a room bar, and made any last-minute telephone calls. In more modern hotels with self-dial telephones in the room, each room has its own unit meter on a panel behind the cashier's desk. She checks the units, multiplies by the rate charged, and adds this last item to the bill.

In some cases the guest may dispute the charges and she must use tact to smooth over such a situation. The guest then pays by cash, credit card or cheque if accepted, or the guest signs the bill which can be sent to his employer. Once the keys are returned, the cashier can then notify the hallporter and housekeeping that the room has been vacated. It is now ready for cleaning, and the guest's luggage can be taken out of the hotel.

▲ The hall porter acts as a kind of information service and keeps keys for guests who have gone out for the day.

Advance reservations clerk

In some hotels, this job comes under the reception department; in others it is a behind-the-scenes job.

Telephone bookings are entered on cards along with those received by letter. By telephone booking, rooms may only be kept till a certain time, say 6 p.m., when they are released if the guest has not arrived. If the guest wants the room kept after that time he may have to guarantee payment, so that if he does not turn up, the hotel is not left with empty, unpaid-for rooms.

▼ Guests are met by the hotel doorman. His uniform recalls that of the coachman in times gone by.

Advance reservations personnel know of bookings for months ahead, how many rooms may be blocked off for redecoration, large groups or conferences. Each booking made is marked off in a large diary and any cancellations are noted. Those working in advance bookings must know every detail of the hotel, from the price of a meal to the time the bars close as well as all the room rates, of course.

Much more information is needed when dealing with bookings for banquets. The reservations clerk will need to know, for instance, how much a band will cost, the cost of banqueting menus, how big the rooms are and how many can be seated for a wedding breakfast, how much flowers will cost and where to get a toastmaster.

The job of the advance reservations clerk is made easier by the use of computers and telex machines. However, a small hotel may only have a large diary and will simply enter bookings in pencil.

The Holiday Inns hotel group was the first with a world-wide computer system, *Holidex*, which gives instant confirmation of whether rooms are available in any of their hotels anywhere in the world. The operator presses buttons for the number and type of rooms required, say, in Barbados or Birmingham. The message is relayed via Memphis, USA, the computer's headquarters, and in seconds a green light indicates that those rooms are available. If the rooms are not available, the machine types out a list of the nearest alternative hotels. The sale is confirmed by pressing another button.

To make sure the hotel is running at a profit, it is vital to keep a close watch on advance bookings. Each hotel has to rely on the fact that a certain percentage of guests will not turn up, and keeps information on other nearby hotels with spare rooms in case of overbooking.

In slow periods one of the day's first tasks is to call the hotel booking agencies at airports and other terminals and tell them what rooms are available on that day. Reservations clerks need to be tidy, accurate, have neat hand-writing and work under pressure. They may also take restaurant reservations by telephone.

Hall porter

The hall porter must have a good knowledge of the area surrounding the hotel and be able to cope with all kinds of requests and arrangements.

The hall porter ushers in guests and looks after their luggage, delivering and collecting it from their rooms. In some hotels, he may go to airports to collect lost luggage.

In some hotels the hall porter may be responsible for handing out guest keys, and late at night will order morning papers and arrange alarm calls. In smaller hotels at night, he will even look after the switchboard, check in any very late arrivals and act as a security officer and room service porter.

How the kitchen is organized

▲ In a special area, the cheese board for the meal serving is set out. In the background is the sweet trolley of cold desserts which will be pushed around the dining room tables.

The atmosphere of a large hotel kitchen is 'organized chaos'. When full meal service is at its height, everyone must work quickly together so that customers are not kept waiting for their food. All this takes a lot of preparation, planning, and training, and the kitchen staff must work together as a team. No one should ever take a kitchen job if they are introverted, shy or nervous. Nor is it the place for those who are weak or prone to illness. Although more women are becoming cooks and chefs, it takes physical strength and skill to chop meat and vegetables correctly and to lift heavy copper stock pots, perhaps containing 20 gallons of hot liquid along with hefty meat bones.

Working in a kitchen is hot and hectic. Even in a modern air-conditioned kitchen, the stove area temperature can be 85-90°F. Accidents can and do happen; scalds and cuts are the most frequent. Hygiene levels have to be high and kitchens are subject to inspection by public health officers at any time. Although high standards of hygiene are a matter of principle for most hotels, some kitchens sometimes fall short of the standards required and can promptly be shut down.

The starched white uniform worn by professional cooks is traditional but its design is totally practical. It is worn for comfort and safety rather than showing off. The tall white cotton hat – *la toque blanche* – is designed to allow cool circulation of air on the head while keeping hair out of the food. A flat cap would be too hot.

Cooks wear a white 'cowboy-style' cotton cloth knotted round their neck or hanging from a jacket

The equipment of a hotel kitchen

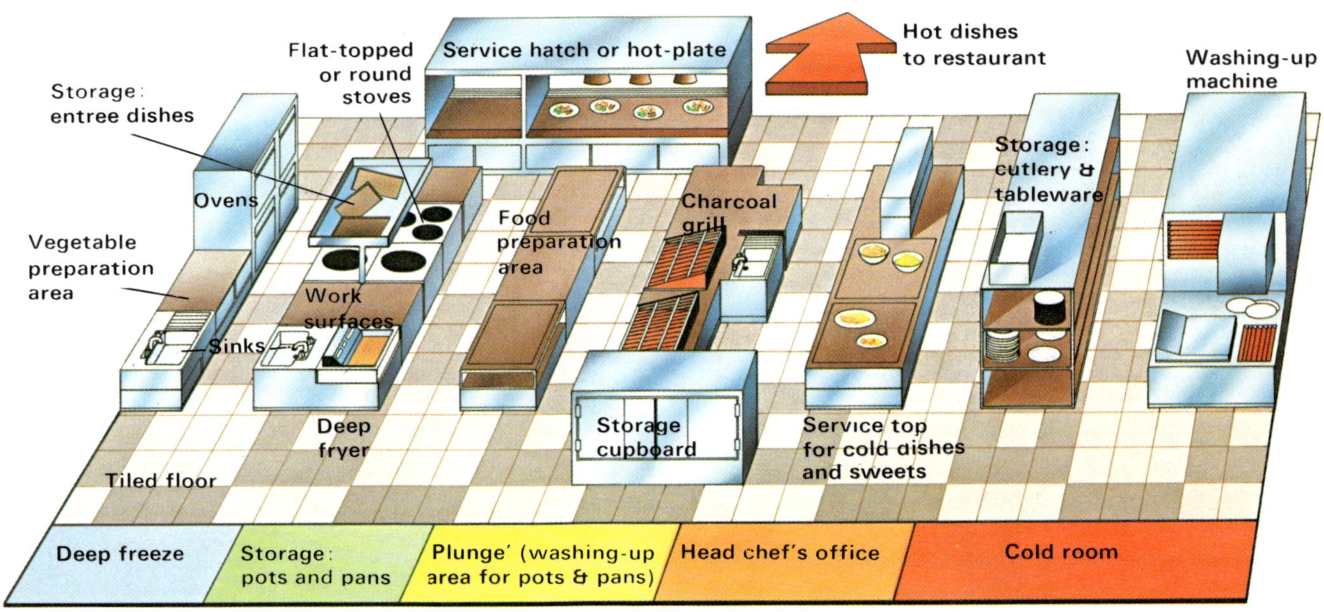

pocket. This is to wipe the sweat from their faces as they work. The cotton jacket is double-breasted to help protect the body when leaning over hot stoves and pans for long periods and to reduce the risk of scalding. The jacket should be long and have a thick apron down to the knees at least to minimize scalds. Cotton trousers are the most cool and comfortable for the kitchen.

Shoes are also important for any worker who has to stand for long periods. A famous chef at a top London hotel advises kitchen staff to 'wear the best brogue-style shoes you can afford with leather soles and uppers (not rubber), or a pair of clogs. Keep a spare pair to change into during the shift'.

The chef is supreme boss in his own kitchen. He interviews and keeps an eye on new trainees and has a deputy to help him. In a large hotel, the head chef and his deputy would have *sous chefs* assigned to different restaurants. The *chefs de partie* are each responsible for a certain section of food preparation such as roasts, vegetables, sauces or pastries. Below them come *commis chefs* and trainee *commis chefs*.

The new entrant will find himself assigned to a section of the kitchen. He must bring with him his own four knives which he will use throughout his working life. A chef can tell if someone else has used his knife; to borrow or steal another's knife is one of the worst 'crimes' of a kitchen.

At the end of his training, the trainee will become a *commis* or assistant chef, working under the direction of a *chef de partie*. Once the *commis* has gained enough experience in this type of cookery, he moves on to another *chef de partie* specializing in another type of food. In this way, the trainee gains experience of all aspects of food preparation and may then apply for a position as *chef de partie* in another hotel.

▼ A trainee chef receives advice from the *chef de partie* he works for. In this case it is the *chef rôtisseur*, who deals with the preparation of various kinds of meat.

Who's who in the kitchen

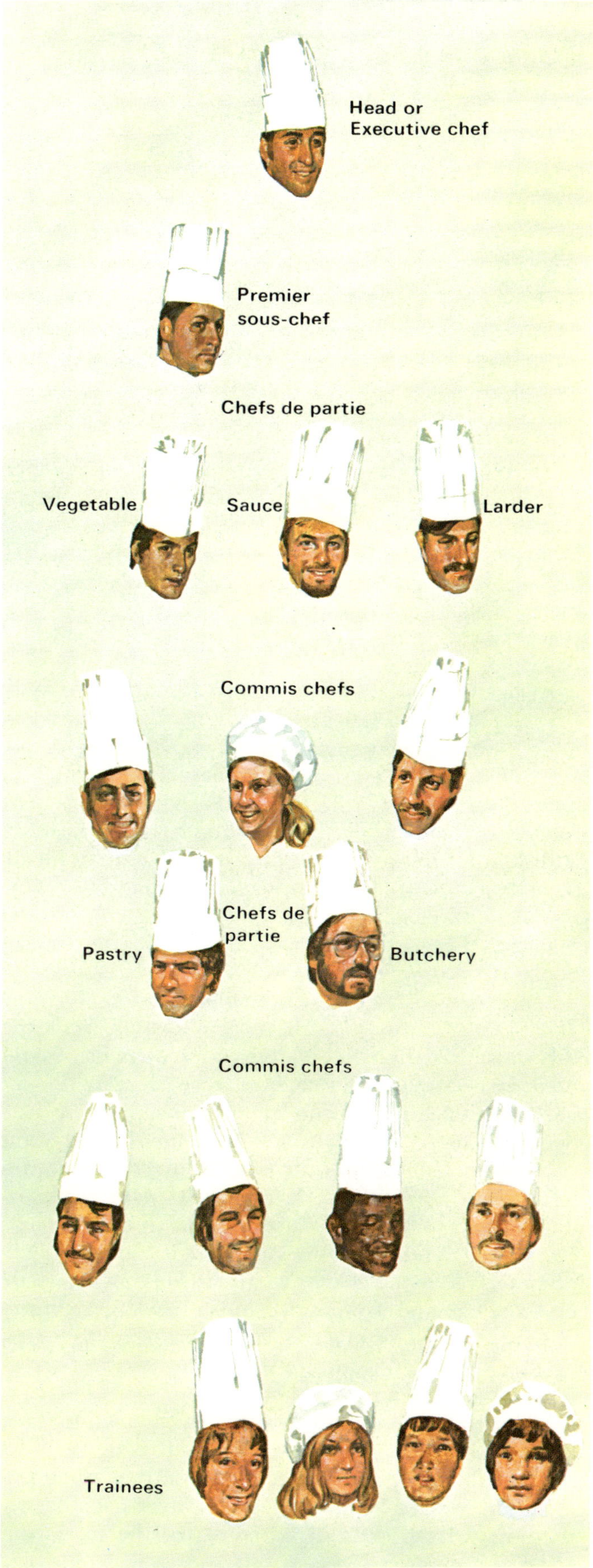

Planning the hotel's meals

Meal planning is the chef's expertise that makes or breaks a hotel's reputation for food. The chef works to an annual budget and must estimate the cost of menus so that they include seasonal variations in the prices of fresh ingredients. He must also know whether the hotel guests are businessmen, rich travellers, budgeting families, or foreign groups perhaps, who may require special meals.

Big hotel groups may have a recipe manual for their chefs to follow. The chef must also know about medical and religious diets for guests who need certain types of food. The personality of the hotel or its location should, if possible, be reflected in the dishes available on the menu. This means that the chef must be aware of local markets and produce and watch out for new foodstuffs coming into season.

Recipes are worked out and costed over a year so that the hotel can estimate its profit margins and can budget for kitchen equipment, fuel, and wages. About 40% of a dish's menu price is the actual cost of the food. Depending on the size of the hotel, recipes can be worked out for one or a hundred servings. In addition to restaurant meals, special costed menus have to be produced in advance for banquets, conferences and private parties.

The chef needs to have two 'bibles' or basic reference books, to work with: *Le Répertoire de La Cuisine* by Saulnier (translated into English) and Herring's *Dictionary of Classical and Modern Cookery*. These give the classical definitions of the many ways of cooking basic foods and which sauces to serve them in.

Most kitchens will order their food supplies at least one week ahead. Hotels usually have their own dry and cold stores, from which the kitchen takes deliveries of items as it needs them. Each *chef de partie* will give daily orders to the chef of the items he thinks he needs. Items such as liqueurs and wines, needed in the preparation of sauces and other dishes, are kept locked in the chef's office, and are handed out to cooks on request.

In an emergency, if a chef runs short of an ingredient or a guest demands an unusual dish, he can 'borrow' from the chef of a nearby hotel.

There should be no 'left-overs' in the well-planned kitchen. The chef should be able to estimate the daily eating habits of his customers and use only as much food as he thinks will be eaten. Any left-overs, such as the trimmings from sides of salmons, will be made into patés and mousses.

▼ As well as being able to create many different dishes, a chef must be aware of cost, since food is an expensive item in the hotel budget. Training leaflets help the trainee chef with ideas of how to make the most economical and appetising use of food.

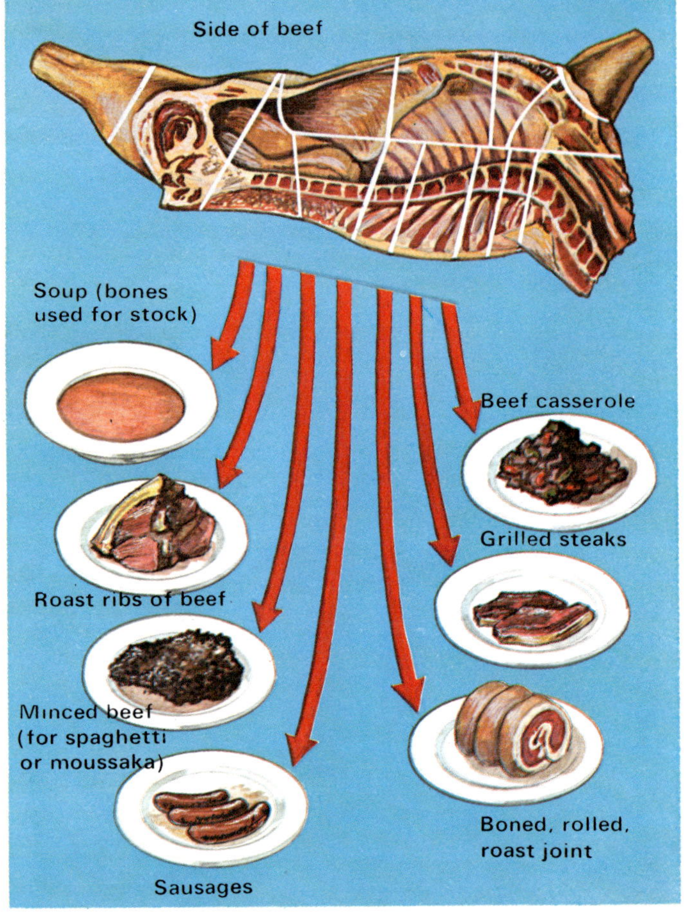

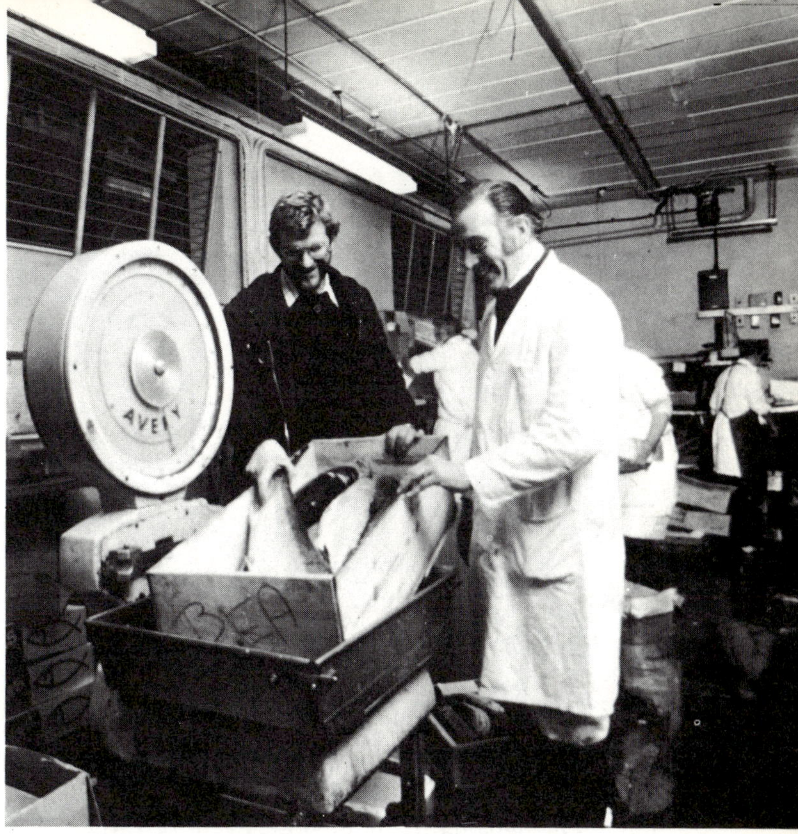

A hotel's weekly food

A large hotel's weekly food bill runs into five figures. The following are some of the items the chef puts down on his weekly shopping list to run two restaurants, a coffee shop and room service for its several hundred guests:

3000 lbs ribs of beef
700 lbs leg of beef
260 lbs beef fillet
1000 lbs leg of pork
1000 lbs leg of lamb
144 honeydew melons
22,000 bread rolls
115 gallons cooking oil
200 avocados
110 lbs French beans
1100 lbs potatoes
100 lbs coffee
9000 eggs
380 lbs fresh butter
38 gallons double cream
25 sides of smoked salmon
4998 pints of milk
148 Dover soles
8400 prawns

▼ Hotel storemen unload a delivery of goods at the hotel loading bays. Fresh perishable goods are delivered daily and dry goods once a week or as required.

The storemen check off the goods and make sure everything that was ordered has been delivered.

▲ The good chef knows what is seasonally available from the markets. Here an executive chef looks at fresh fish at London's Billingsgate market.

By buying produce himself, the chef can ensure that the hotel's guests receive the freshest and best of food.

The kitchen at work

In large hotel kitchens, staff work in two shifts, covering the day from 8 a.m. until midnight. In smaller hotels, the staff may take a break in the late afternoon between main meals when the hotel is quiet. Breakfast service in large hotels may be separate from the main kitchen, and in a few hotels a 24-hour room service or coffee shop food service may be maintained. Breakfast staff start work at about 6.30 a.m. Trays will probably have been prepared the previous day with bacon rashers, sausages and halved tomatoes. These can be cooked first and kept hot till needed.

The chef arrives at about 8 a.m. His first job is to look at night reports, and to check his diary to see if there are any banquets or special meals to be attended to. Then he makes up the orders for the next day's meals. Paper work and accounts take up more of the morning, with interruptions from *sous chefs* with problems and ideas. The chef must then check with the reservations desk to see if there are any special orders for groups of guests coming in up to three months ahead so that food can be ordered and any special menus prepared. The bigger the kitchen, the less actual cooking the chef may do. But all chefs make quite sure their recipes are carried out just the way they wish.

Ordering a meal
The waiter takes the guest's orders. All have ordered a different dish.

The chef in charge calls out the orders to the various *chefs de partie*.

The chefs prepare their own dish and bring it to the chef in charge, who checks it.

The waiter collects the dishes he has ordered.

◀ Each morning the decorative desserts for the sweet trolley, which have been made the previous day, are finished off.

▶ The waiters come in from the dining room bringing menu orders. When the food is ready, they collect it from the chefs over a special counter, and take it to the diners.

▼ In a busy kitchen, it is important that there should be enough clean cutlery, china and glasses to serve everyone. Modern hotels have big washing up machines and the 'plunge' is the area in the kitchen for washing up pots and pans.

▶ One of the first jobs a trainee cook will learn in a hotel kitchen is how to prepare vegetables. As well as preparing potatoes cleanly and evenly, he will learn the correct way to cut onions and cauliflower.

Tours are made in the kitchen to check on hygiene and safety and to make sure that *sous chefs* are following the recipes given to them. Menus for the day are given out and the food preparation is begun. Vegetables are cleaned, peeled, and blanched in boiling water and put away in the fridge till needed for cooking. Special types of meat, such as venison, will have been soaked in herbs and wine for two days before cooking. Salads are made up and meat is cut into joints or chopped if necessary. Gateaux and bases for cold sweets are made the day before and decorated and finished in the morning.

Arguments and mistakes often happen in the kitchen, of course. There may also be complaints: a diner sends back an underdone steak, or vegetables that are badly cooked, and another might complain that his food is cold. Hopefully, though, there will be praise and the chef is called to the dining room for a drink with the guests. By 3 p.m. things are quieter and it is time to prepare the evening meal and food for the next day. There is always plenty to do in a kitchen. The whole process is repeated in the evening, when dinner service begins at 7 p.m. After midnight, staff come in to wash the floors, surfaces, stoves, pots and pans.

Kitchen staff

The hierarchy of a large hotel kitchen is still very classical. Modern equipment has made the cooking process much more streamlined and efficient, although staff duties themselves have not changed much over the years. This basic pattern, which is adjusted according to the size and type of hotel, is very international so that a cook soon finds himself at home whichever country he may be in. French terminology is universally much used and knowledge of French classical cuisine is essential.

Chef

The chef is the supreme boss over anyone who comes into his kitchen. In a large hotel, he may have an immediate superior, the Food and Beverage Manager, who in turn reports to the hotel manager. In smaller hotels, the chef works closely with the manager on a day-to-day basis.

The chef is responsible for an annual budget which covers food buying, menus, kitchen equipment, staff wages and uniforms. A food order can run to as much as £1000 a day for a large kitchen.

He prepares recipes and menus of his own and teaches these to the chefs he is training. Kitchen equipment and its repair is also his concern, as are safety, hygiene, security and training. He must also be able to relieve any of his chefs who are ill.

Most chefs will plan menus usually three months ahead: banqueting menus must also be prepared and be attractive to clients. The chef works closely with the various restaurant head waiters and checks on how the dishes are liked by the public.

A chef may visit local markets occasionally or as frequently as he can, where he can then get new ideas for recipes. By talking to a fishmonger or butcher in person, he can have meat or fish specially cut to his requirements. The chef will also represent his hotel on various culinary courses and displays on a world-wide basis. Sometimes chefs are sent abroad to make exchange food festivals with other hotels.

Sous chef

There are under', or *sous* chefs, in charge of each restaurant in a large hotel, one for each shift worked. The *sous chefs* can be responsible for the *à la carte* restaurant or grill room, usually the most expensive of the hotel's restaurants. Other *sous chefs* will look after the carvery, the coffee shop, and there will also be a *sous chef* in charge of banquets.

Chef de partie

The *chefs de partie* (section chefs) each have responsibility for a part of the cooking pattern of the kitchen. On the way up the kitchen careers ladder, cooks will change round the different sections so that at the end they have a complete knowledge of every aspect of professional cookery.

The *chefs de partie* also have responsibility for helping to train new young cooks, watching their progress and making reports to the head chef. The *chefs de partie* cover such areas as fish, vegetables, sauces, grills, larder (cold foods) and pastries.

There will also be a *chef tournant*, whose job it is to take over another chef's job if he is sick or absent. A *chef tournant* has to make himself especially familiar with the head chef's recipes and ways of working so that he can take over any section at short notice and not make any mistakes in making up a dish or presenting it.

First commis chef

This is the assistant to the *chef de partie*, and a first *commis* will be attached to each of the sections in the kitchen. First *commis chefs* also have a hand in training new staff.

Trainee cook

The trainees are school leavers, usually on block release from technical college. Meals and a uniform will be provided. At the end of a shift, the trainee will have to clean his own chopping board, shelf and preparation area. He will also have to see to the correct rotation of food within his section fridge.

◀ Young cooks learn the correct way to prepare good food professionally at a catering training college. They can attend day classes or enrol for full-time courses.

The work is hard, and most trainees start with vegetable preparation. They learn how to peel and 'turn', or shape, potatoes, how to chop onions correctly, and other basic skills as they move around the kitchen sections. The chef may also sometimes allocate them special test dishes to make up.

Strong wrists and plenty of common sense are definite assets to the trainee cook. In some kitchens there is the opportunity to learn the skills of butter or ice carving for buffets and banquets, or make elaborate dishes for displays and competitions at hotel exhibitions.

People intending to train in kitchen work should be artistic and know that presentation of food in a hotel is not just a matter of cooking it well: they must know how to arrange it appetisingly and how to garnish it with attractively cut vegetables. Every good chef knows that food must please the eye, the nose, and the taste in that order.

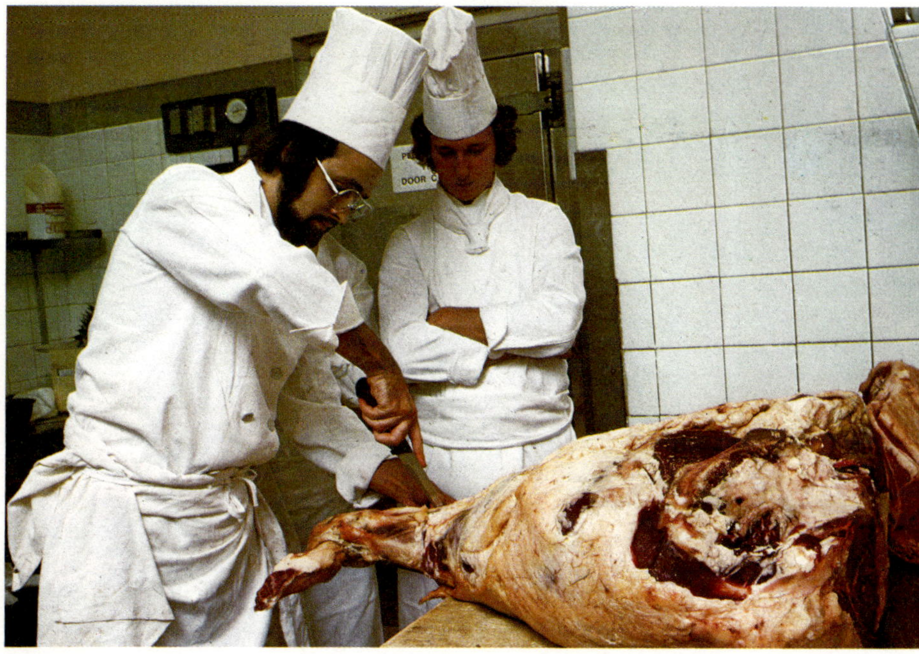

▲ A young cook is shown the different cuts of meat. This leg of beef will be roasted whole and served in a hotel carvery restaurant where guests carve the meat themselves.

Breakfast cook

In some hotels, a cook may be employed to prepare breakfast only. The job includes making the breakfast dishes to the set menu and placing them on plates ready for service. The cook will be responsible for clearing up equipment afterwards and looking after the stove used. Previous experience is not always necessary and this can be a part-time job.

Breakfast supervisor

The breakfast supervisor may come under the housekeeping department. This person checks that breakfast trays go to bedrooms on time, are correctly laid and the china clean. The breakfast supervisor checks on all the breakfasts from the floor service areas, makes sure that the orders are correct and that the bills have been made out.

Coffee shop cook

Special cooks may be required for the hotel coffee shop. This is a restaurant with lengthy hours of opening and which serves lighter, international snack-style dishes. The cooks work an early or late shift and need little experience to cook service meals such as grills, omelettes, pancakes and fried breakfast-style dishes. Breakfast may also be served in this room instead of in the main dining room.

Service assistant

These are, as the name implies, assistants to cooks in various areas away from the main kitchen. No previous experience is usually required. Duties include making tea, coffee, toast, preparing a food counter for service, and cleaning cookery areas. Shifts are worked according to the department which is being served. Salads, sandwiches, teas, and hors d'oeuvres preparation may be included.

Day and night cook

In hotels where room or floor service is provided, cooks are required on shift systems covering 24 hours. A year's experience is usually asked for in working as a 'fast food' cook. The work mainly consists of making snacks, sandwiches, and salads.

Kitchen porter and storeman

The work consists of cleaning the kitchen generally and collecting foods and goods from the hotel stores as required by the cooks. No previous experience is necessary. In some large hotels storemen and porters will come under the Essential Services department.

Storemen need to have good reading and writing ability and be able to keep clear and accurate check records of the in and out flow of the goods in their charge.

Cleaning staff

Large kitchens need cleaners, who usually come in at night or when the kitchen is free from service. They must clean all floors and major equipment to the standards of hygiene required.

Plateman

No previous experience is necessary. On shifts, platemen load dirty crockery and glassware brought in by the waiters into dish washing machines and unload and stack dishes when clean.

In the dining room

The waiter and waitress in the hotel dining room must learn several basic skills. First of all, of course, they must learn how to lay a table correctly and how to serve food properly and take a menu order. They must also learn which condiments go with which dish; for example, the difference between French and English mustards and when to use them. Apart from this, every waiter and waitress should have some knowledge of French, which is the language internationally used in cooking, so that they will be able to understand the menu and be able to explain dish descriptions to guests.

Tact and patience are also required with difficult or indecisive customers, especially when the waiter has several tables to deal with at once, and must try to give each one as much attention as possible. As in the kitchen, the dining room staff must work as a team, especially at peak times, to ensure the smooth running of the restaurant.

Not only must the dining room staff be neat, clean and pleasant, the guests may also have to be correctly dressed and keep to certain rules. Many hotel grill rooms, for instance, will not accept a man without a tie or jacket and one or two still turn away women wearing trousers. Some top hotels even keep a supply of jackets and ties to lend to guests.

▲ Guests may have to wear jackets and ties in certain hotel restaurants. Rather than turn a guest away, the restaurant manager offers a selection of ties kept specially by the hotel.

How to lay a table

Some guests try and trick a restaurant out of the price. They complain that the food is bad or badly cooked. The restaurant manager will need to handle the matter with a great deal of tact, of course, but he may have to ask them why they continued to eat it all. Some customers deliberately try to cause trouble, and the restaurant manager must investigate complaints to make sure they are genuine. In some cases, it may simply be a case of misunderstanding – for example in the case of a customer who orders his steak to be cooked 'saignant' or 'rare', not knowing what the terms mean. But if the complaint seems deserved, the restaurant manager will offer an alternative dish or a drink on the house and make sure the customer is happy before he leaves.

In smarter hotels, the main dining room will have 'silver service', which means that food is served from silver-plate platters using a spoon and a fork held in one hand. Learning to cope with serving this way is tricky. Trainees often practise with stale rolls, dried peas or paper clips but the most difficult test is to cope with elastic bands. This simulates green beans, spaghetti and spinach – all tricky items.

All tips go into a box, known as a *tronc*, which is opened by the head waiter. The money is divided out between the staff, according to their work status.

▲ More modern hotels may try to give their restaurant an individual touch. Here, the waiters' uniforms are made to match the colour scheme of the dining room.

▼ In some hotels, especially resort hotels, lunchtime may be a little less formal. Here, guests serve themselves with a little help from the restaurant manager.

A waiter's life

Waiting at table looks deceptively simple. All you have to do, it seems, is carry a plate, put it on a table, and later clear it away. But have you ever tried carrying even two hot, full plates without spilling anything or burning your fingers? Have you ever tried to draw a cork from a bottle smoothly just by holding it in one hand, not putting it between the legs and heaving?

The skills of a waiter are learnt on the job and come basically from practice. They say it takes at least two years in a good restaurant to learn all the skills of high class service. But techniques can be learnt much quicker.

Waiters can attend special courses to learn the tricks of the trade. They learn such things as how to prepare lemon wedges for fish dishes. The waiter must make sure that a membrane is left on both sides of the wedge, so when squeezed, the juice runs down onto the plate and not straight into the diner's eye!

When taking orders, the waiter relies on a good memory to remember who ordered what. Experienced waiters with large tables make diagrams on the order pad. The correct cutlery must be put out as needed – soup spoons, fish knives and forks or steak knives. The waiter must keep his orders neat and correct so they are completely legible by the chef, and must not create trouble by blaming the kitchen for mistakes. However, battles in the kitchen may be inevitable, and a waiter who has been particularly troublesome may be rewarded by being given an empty platter under a cover – hardly the way to get the best tips.

▲ Often hot dishes of food are brought in on trays and separated by metal rings. Here a waiter removes a pile of empty dishes.

▼ 'Waiter, there's a hair in my soup!' The waiter notes complaints and passes them on to the restaurant manager.

▼ Some dishes are cooked over a lamp next to the table and may be flamed in alchohol – sometimes with disastrous results!

► As well as learning basic skills, such as serving and carving, the waiter must also be polite and attentive to the guest.

But in most establishments, the most important task for the waiter is collecting hot food and carrying it to the table. You cannot bring just one plate at a time while guests sit over cooling food. Four fully loaded plates can be carried at once. One plate goes between thumb and forefinger (with the thumb on the rim not in the food), the next between forefinger and the three remaining fingers, a third in the crook of the arm and the fourth in the other hand.

When clearing away, the expert waiter takes the dirtiest plate first. All the better if it is a woman's as they are served and cleared first. A good waiter can clear up to eight dirty plates at once. There is even a correct way to remove an ashtray: it should be covered with the hand or a clean ashtray. This is not for show but because a full ashtray whisked away will scatter all over the table. And the waiter must also know the art of removing a dirty cloth and putting on a new one in one slick movement in front of diners without uncovering the bare table.

The traditional waiter's outfit is black tails and a starched shirt with a false front tied on. The trainee waiter often wears a white cotton jacket, black trousers, white shirt and bow tie. Waitresses may wear a black dress and white apron, a hotel uniform, or, for special banquets, may find themselves dressed in period costume.

► Very often a guest likes to have a drink or a meal in his room. Room service waiters see that everything is loaded onto the trolly and deliver the food to the guest's room.

▼ Waiters must know something of religious and medical diets.

▼ As part of their 'social training' waiters should place the chair correctly and firmly behind the guests as they sit down.

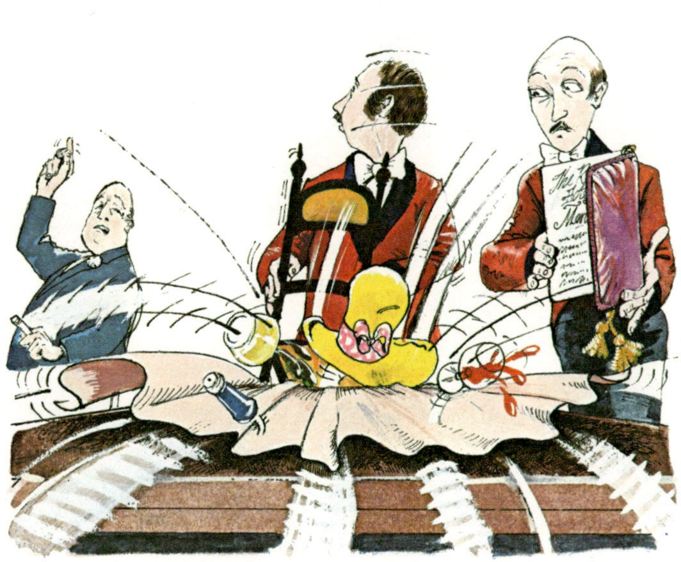

Serving drinks in the hotel

The dining room is the province of the wine waiter and he must know everything there is to know about wine. It is important to store and serve wines at the correct temperature. Red wine is served at room temperature and white wines are served chilled. The drier the wine the more it should be chilled. The wine waiter makes sure that good red wines are brought up from the cellar well ahead of the main course. Then, with the guest's permission, he opens the bottle gently so as not to disturb any sediment. It is then placed in a 'cradle' and allowed to 'breathe' during the first course.

When bringing wine to the table, the wine waiter presents it to the host, showing him the label so he knows the right bottle has been brought. On taking out the cork, the waiter should first smell the wine to make sure it is not 'corked' or has a musty, bitter smell or taste. He will then pour a little wine in the host's glass for him to taste and approve. The good waiter, when pouring, remembers to fill glasses only two thirds full, never to the top. This destroys the bouquet or aroma.

The wine waiter will also advise on what to drink with different dishes. Most hotels now standardize their glasses to a basic goblet or tulip shaped glass, but the waiter must still know the right shaped glasses to use for champagne, red and white wines, liqueurs and brandies. He may also have to decant – usually by straining through fine muslin – a vintage red wine or a port and must pour both slowly and carefully.

▲ Sharing the *tronc*. The *tronc* is the collective box of tips received by dining room staff. Methods vary, but the amount is usually shared out by the head waiter to staff according to their seniority.

▼ Some of the larger hotels keep a well-stocked wine cellar and a full-time cellarman may be employed.

Hotel bartenders have been responsible for inventing some of the world's most famous drinks. The dry martini was created by a hotel barman and the 'Singapore Sling' came first from Singapore's famous and elegant Raffles Hotel. Barmen need to know how to make up about five hundred standard cocktails. If they are asked to make up a drink they have not heard of, they refer to books such as *The Bartenders' Guide* to help them.

The hotel barman should have many talents. First of all, of course, he needs to know which drinks and brands to stock, and in what quantities. He should be able to serve different beers so that the sediment does not get into the glass and he should have an artistic flair, to be able to create decorative effects with lemon, orange, cherries, mint and borage sprigs. There is also a correct way to use a cocktail shaker and every barman should know how much crushed ice to use in a drink. Sometimes he may even be called upon to make up a non-alcoholic drink like a 'Pussyfoot' for a child. The good experienced barman will know how to create that extra effect by putting a little white of egg in a drink to make it froth at the top or adding a dash of Grand Marnier to draw out the flavour of a champagne cocktail.

More than this, though, they have to be good listeners and hear the tales the customers tell them over the bar. They may even have to act as doctors and mix drinks and offer sympathy for upset stomachs and aching hangovers. The cures that most barmen recommend are Fernet Branca or an Underberg Shot; others will offer 'Buck's Fizz', a mixture of champagne and orange juice, or a 'Bloody Mary' (vodka and tomato juice) as good pick-me-ups. For a cold they may mix rum, brandy, or whisky with hot water, lemon juice, sugar and cloves.

▲ A wine waiter should always show the bottle of wine and its label to the customer before opening it. This ensures that the right wine has been brought from the cellar.

▼ Barmen are skilful at mixing cocktails and know how to prepare hundreds of different drinks.

Restaurant and bar staff

The typical hotel dining room is organized like the kitchen and many of the terms used are also French. For example, the senior waiter is called a *chef de rang*. This is nothing to do with cooking but comes from the French word *chef* meaning 'leader' or 'chief'. The *rang* is a section of tables for which the waiter is responsible. Below him work the *commis* or junior waiters. At the top of the hierarchy are the restaurant manager, responsible to the food and beverage manager, and the head waiter.

Restaurant manager

The restaurant manager has overall responsibility for one dining room in the hotel. In some cases, he will inform his staff of the dishes of the day and give details of any VIP's coming to dine. He will oversee the bookings, making sure that regular customers have their usual tables. He will check that tables and equipment are up to standard and order extra china or food items as needed.

Cleanliness and safety procedures are also his responsibility. The restaurant manager must deal with any complaint and also take responsibility for refusing a guest entry to the dining room. Depending on the size of the hotel, he may escort diners to tables and take orders.

Head waiter

The senior or head waiter may also act as restaurant manager in a smaller hotel. He supervises all the waiters' work and makes sure no customers are kept waiting. In some cases, he takes orders, particularly from those guests selecting dishes over drinks in the bar. It is the head waiter's job to divide out the *tronc* of tips between the waiters.

Chef de rang

These are senior waiters who advise guests on the menu, take the orders and usually wear a more formal uniform than the *commis* waiter. When the food arrives from the kitchen, the *chef de rang* will serve this from platters at the table. If any flambé dishes, such as *steak diane* or *crepes suzette*, are ordered, the senior waiter will cook these at the table. Finally, the *chef de rang* must check the tables for presentation and make sure that the right cutlery and china have been put out.

Commis waiter

The *commis* is the trainee waiter. He takes his instructions from the *chef de rang* and he will learn the job both by working and taking part in the hotel industry training schemes. In a top class restaurant, the *commis* waiter will be responsible for an average of six tables.

He will place items such as flowers on the table, replace candles if used, put out clean ashtrays and hotel matches. He should also check the equipment on the sideboard of his 'station' or section of the dining room. He will make up mustards, put peppercorns in the mill, prepare lemon wedges for fish dishes and ensure that serving spoons, forks, redcurrant jelly, mint sauce and other items are ready to hand. He will set out glasses and bring in plates for the cold courses. Finally, he brings in rolls from the kitchen, places them on plates or in a serving basket and makes up the coffee in the still room near the kitchen.

Like the other waiters, the *commis* waiter attends the daily briefing session to discuss the menu of the day so that he knows what is being offered and how it is cooked. During the meal service, the job of the *commis* waiter is to fetch and carry. He takes food orders from the *chef de rang* to the kitchen.

Learning simple tricks, like placing a sprig of parsley on a well-done steak, helps him to identify which steak is which if several are ordered together at different degrees of cooking. The *commis* waiter collects and clears each course and clears ashtrays as needed. If there are two sittings in the dining room, he will clear the table and reset with clean linen between servings.

General waiter and waitress

In smaller hotels, coffee shops, simpler-styled restaurants and breakfast rooms, a school leaver may start as a waiter or waitress and have to do more order taking, bill making up, and serving earlier than the *commis* waiter in a large hotel. Service is usually called 'plate service', and the food, or at least the meat or fish, is pre-placed on a china plate in the kitchen.

Many hotels issue work plans for service to help trainees. It may look easy to serve food, but when people are paying for service they expect it to be done smoothly and professionally. Hotels even

▶ Waitresses may often be required to wear period costume or a special uniform.

lay down rules for serving potatoes! When serving a salad, for example, the waiter needs to find out from the diner whether he wants it mixed or plain green and the type of dressing required. Then the salad must be mixed and carefully arranged, to be placed finally at the top right of the main plate with an extra fork.

The waiter will also be serving children and may have to get special foods and small portions and arrange a high chair or cushion for the child.

Wine waiter

In some hotels the waiter may have to deal with wine service as well. But in larger hotels this is a separate job. The wine waiter is responsible for offering aperitifs while guests are reading the menu. He then returns when the dishes have been chosen and helps the guests to choose an appropriate wine. He then collects the bottles and sets out the right glasses.

The diner does not expect to have to wait for his wine, so the waiter ensures it is served in good time for each course — white with the fish and red with meat. Of course, the glasses must not be dirty or chipped.

In addition to wines, the wine waiter serves mineral waters on request, and at the end of the meal brings round a liqueur trolley or fetches drinks from the bar to order. He must know how to warm a brandy 'balloon' (glass), the correct legal measures, how to create coffee drinks with liqueurs in them, and make *frappé* drinks with crushed ice. He also looks after the restaurant's supply of cigars.

Many wine waiters are members of the Guild of Sommeliers, an international organization which gives extra information and training. Many of the wine and brewing companies also run special courses for wine waiters and barmen.

Barman

Many barmen begin service life as dining room waiters, but others start straight away in the bar assisting the head barman. In hotels, bars open early for the residents. A typical day in the bar will start at about 9 a.m. with cleaning and restocking. Glasses are cleaned and rescued from other parts of the hotel where guests may have taken them. Fresh ingredients, such as orange and lemon juice, orange and lemon slices, egg whites, Tabasco and Worcester sauces must be assembled. Plenty of ice is also needed – on a summer's day up to two hundred kilos may be used in a big hotel bar.

Bars are also subject to hygiene inspection. The barman must also be aware of the various laws involved in his trade. For example, measures must be legally exact. Non residents must not be served out of usual licensing hours and under-age people not served. If drunken incidents break out, the barman can call on the security officer for help.

Many barmen belong to the Bartenders' Guild which provides information and training, and organizes 'cocktail inventing' competitions. Being a barman needs more know-how than dispensing a scotch and soda. He must know how to make up cocktails, many of which have such colourful names as 'daisies', 'flips', or 'highballs'. This may take a long time, since there are estimated to be about twelve thousand cocktail recipes in the world!

Room service waiter

This waiter takes telephone orders from guests' rooms, takes trays or hot tables with food, drinks, baby foods or snacks to the room. He also looks after the room service kitchen and its contents and sends bills to the cashiers.

▼ An evening meal is sent up to a guest's room. Some hotels operate a 24-hour service.

Conferences and banquets

Selling as much accommodation as possible is the aim of every hotel. Most hotels hope to fill about seventy to eighty per cent of their rooms over a year to make the business profitable. Running a hotel nowadays is more than just expecting a weary and thankful traveller to turn up on the hotel doorstep; accommodation has to be sold hard. No hotel likes to be too dependent on one source of customer and tries to encourage different categories of guests, sometimes at reduced rates.

According to its location, a hotel defines whether it wants business, holiday, full-rate or group travellers. In off-season times, special bargain rates and extra inclusive attractions such as hobby interests are offered. At all times though, conferences and special meetings are good business.

The Sales Manager and his staff may work for one large hotel or a group of several. Among other things, he must supervise the preparation of sales leaflets and brochures and brief an advertising agency on the way he thinks the hotel should be presented to the public. Occasionally, he may travel abroad selling accommodation and appointing hotel representatives in major countries so that travel agents can make reservations locally and quickly.

Many large hotels have a separate conference and banquets department. The staff contact businessmen's secretaries and give them details of the hotel facilities. Satisfied customers who come back a second time and 'word of mouth' recommendations are equally important. Clients who make enquiries are given information packs including accurate dimensions of rooms for functions. When a function is booked, everything is carefully documented so both sides know exactly what has been agreed and to avoid any double-booking.

Hotel functions can be as varied as press launches for a new product, a working session for a group of businessmen, a big annual conference or a society ball. Cocktail parties, fashion shows, even nights of boxing or classical concerts have been put on in hotels. Film producers often use hotels as settings and provided the hotel gets a good image, the sales staff agree. But in all their activities, they have to ensure the ordinary hotel user is not upset by larger parties, noise from a private dinner-dance or lack of attention from busy staff.

◄ The Sales Manageress must try to 'sell' the hotel's conference facilities to the potential customer. In other words, she must convince him that her hotel can provide a better service than its rivals.

◄ A Conference Manager confirms a booking with his secretary. He is responsible for the smooth running of the conference, from supplying audio-visual equipment to making sure that enough food has been ordered.

► On special occasions, such as when VIP's have been invited to a banquet, the hotel manager makes a personal check on the arrangements.

▲ The chef and storekeeper discuss how much food they will need to order for a future banquet.

► Firms may take over an entire suite or floor of a hotel. They may also expect the hotel to provide special equipment, such as microphones and projectors.

▲ Advance preparation is vital when five hundred guests need feeding at the same time.

Special facilities

Hotels can roughly be divided into three types: the city hotel, catering for tours and businessmen, the motel for motorists on brief stop-overs, and the resort hotel. The first real resort hotels were called 'spa' hotels. People stayed in them for pleasure and relaxation rather than out of necessity. These still exist, particularly in Germany, France and Italy, where treatments are given using the health-giving waters. Staff may include medical personnel.

Most city hotels now provide a variety of services and special facilities to tempt the customer. Indoor swimming pools are part of every Holiday Inn, but many hotels have big outdoor pools with attendants. One hotel in Sweden even has underwater stereo for its indoor swimmers!

Sometimes hotels are able to offer all the facilities the guest may need. Banking and currency exchange services are available in many hotel lobbies, and, should the guest wish to buy a souvenir or any items he has forgotten to bring with him, he will find a shop in the reception area stocked with a wide variety of goods from soap and toilet articles to clothes and handbags. The hotel may also run its own hairdressing salon.

Usually, though, these facilities are not actually owned by the hotel, but are given out on a concession basis to outside traders. For example, the tours desk will be run by an outside tour company, which will provide information on tours and arrange visits for the hotel guests. Many tours will be to local places of interest or historical sites, but the tour operator will also provide trips to theatres or concerts.

Sometimes the hotel may provide its own 'hospitality' or 'guest relations' desk, where staff are trained to answer general enquiries and help to smooth out any problems the guest may have. As with all front of house personnel the staff must have tact and patience, and be able to deal with people on all levels.

Sports have become closely associated with many hotels. Fishing hotels tend to be small and isolated with their own or accessible fishing rights and tolerant chefs prepared to cook the catch. Golf hotels such as Gleneagles and Turnberry in Scotland have their own championship golf courses and professional teachers on the staff. In the United States, hotels called 'tennis ranches' are springing up, often founded by tennis stars. Here the day's activity is centred round learning and playing tennis. Sports hotels often have shops supplying equipment as well as professional teachers.

Entertainment is important in resort hotels which may be remote from towns, and hotels may arrange as many entertainments as they can. Caribbean hotels arrange pool-side film and limbo shows, beach barbecues and even crab racing on the beach! In Las Vegas, the huge hotels have built-in theatres for spectacular dinner shows and in many countries casinos are hotel attractions.

◀ Larger hotels may employ a special member of staff trained to give information and deal with guests' problems.

▼ More and more hotels are now providing indoor swimming pools.

▲ Sports have now become closely associated with resort hotels. In some tennis 'ranches', professional tennis players may act as coaches.

► Golfing fanatics can spend weeks playing their favourite sport at special golf hotels. When bad weather stops play there may be films or discussions in the evenings.

► Guests may find interesting souvenirs or everyday necessities provided for them in the hotel shop.

▼ Where possible, a hotel might try to run a hairdressing salon for the convenience of female guests. Outside hairdressers run the business on a 'concession' business.

Staff behind the scenes

To the guest checking in at a large hotel, the pattern of life seems smooth and trouble-free. This is, of course, the impression the hotel wishes to create. A great number of staff are employed to work 'behind the scenes' and will never come into contact with the public. It is up to them to ensure the smooth and efficient running of the hotel.

For instance, one of the more important jobs is to keep the hotel warm and provide plenty of hot water for the guests. This is the job of the hotel engineers, who see to the running of the hotel's huge boilers and make sure they never break down. The hotel staff will also include electricians, carpenters and plumbers, who must be available for twenty-four hours a day in case of emergency, as well as for smaller jobs, such as replacing light bulbs or unblocking drains. It is the job of the works manager to supervise the works maintenance staff and cooperate with other departments, such as housekeeping.

Other essential services which go unnoticed by the hotel guest are the stationery supervisor and the laundry staff. The supply of stationery involves such items as menus, notepaper for the guests' rooms and all stationery required by hotel staff in day-to-day working.

▼ A supply of hot water for washing and heating is vital to the hotel. The engineer must overhaul the boilers regularly to make sure they are in working order.

The stationery supervisor must be aware of banquets and special conferences coming up, since he or she may have to supply 500 menus for the occasion, as well as keeping the stationery room stocked with the normal supply of stationery needed.

In some hotels, laundry may be done on the premises by staff, while other hotels prefer to send it out. In either case, staff will need to be employed to sort out linen and store it, and a female member of staff may also be on hand to do any sewing or mending required.

Security is now becoming an increasing priority for most big hotels with their constantly changing flow of guests. Many often carry large sums of money or travellers' cheques and their best jewels and clothes, and this makes a likely setting for crime of all kinds. More and more hotels are appointing security officers, replacing the old house detective, a character much seen in early American films. Most security officers are ex-policemen and armed servicemen who know how to question suspects and make court appearances. The London Police now have a special hotel squad which is one of the fastest growing divisions.

Security officers, patrolling the hotel all through the day and night, watch for suspicious signs and try and train all other staff to help, particularly in watching for parcels that might contain a bomb. The security officer also looks after and checks fire appliances and supervises money going to and from the hotel's bank.

▼ The advance reservations clerk takes telephone reservations and keeps a record of all bookings. In larger hotels, she must learn how to use telex machines and sometimes even computers to arrange bookings.

▲ Even hotels which have their laundry done by outside firms may employ someone to do basic mending and sorting of linen.

▼ Hotel switchboard operators receive calls from all over the world. They need to locate both guests and staff quickly, often paging them over public address systems.

A hotel manager's day

▼ The manager discusses the day's accounts with the hotel accountant, and any problems are sorted out.

▼ The chef presents his ideas for daily menus, or for a special banquet, for the manager's approval.

▼ A visit from an interior designer requires the manager's opinion on colour schemes or types of wall-paper, and he may also need to know the cost.

▼ Sometimes he will be required to interview personnel for senior management jobs.

▼ He takes an interest in how the food is being prepared, and samples the day's special dish.

▼ An important banquet is being held. The manager will be on hand to see that everything is being prepared according to his wishes.

Hotel management

▲ The front office manager. He is in charge of staff who work in the reception area of the hotel.

Because hotels are such complex places, supplying services for many different nationalities, those in management need all-round experience of all aspects of hotel work, if they are to cope with the many problems that arise in such a self-contained community in twenty-four hours. The manager supervises the different areas of activity and needs to have had experience in accountancy, booking procedure, housekeeping problems, catering and hotel law.

Manager

He is the ultimate boss, who takes responsibility for everything that happens in his hotel. He will hold meetings with departmental heads and regular staff or personnel meetings. He will make inspections of the hotel as he thinks necessary. His day is never the same and is planned out specially. He has to use his time wisely; the hours are long and hard. A manager needs to be a 'jack of all trades': lawyer, safety expert, policeman, chef, accountant, and marketing executive – in all a total businessman.

He needs to know everything, from the latest pay reviews to the best rubbish disposal system. He decides on whether the design of an ashtray should be changed, and briefs staff on what to do if a bomb is found. He investigates complaints, meets VIP's and may have a drink or meal with them. Every day he checks on bookings and occupancy levels.

The job of a manager is international, and many have worked in hotels all over the world. Many managers often assume importance in local community affairs, attending business functions and knowing local mayors and industrial companies. Royalty and heads of state are frequent hotel visitors and the manager must be aware of both etiquette and of security to make sure that their visit is flawless.

He must be able to anticipate a crisis and plan ahead. For example, if a power cut is likely, he orders candles and lamps well ahead, checks fire risks, prints notices for guests in several languages, and works on menus that will need the least power.

In smaller hotels, the manager will be more personally involved in the day-to-day running, discussing menus with the chef, checking on bookings and even taking over staff duties if someone is ill.

Assistant manager

The assistant manager deputises for the manager and will be responsible for overall events in the hotel. An assistant, or duty manager, will be on duty twenty-four hours a day, sleeping in the hotel in a spare room. In smaller and resort hotels, he usually lives in. Duty managers are those who have finished their college training and are learning the practical side the hard way, being put in charge on a day-long shift.

They have to estimate bookings, decide whether to sell more and risk overbooking or let a double room go at a single-price. They deal with complaints, liaise with security, and listen to staff problems. It may sound fascinating to be in charge of what amounts to a 'mini city', but it means possibly dealing with a fire, a bathroom flood, a death, assisting the police in enquiries or surviving a power cut. Sometimes they all seem to happen at once!

Managing a hotel brings many rewards, however. It means being in charge of a well-run, attractive hotel to which famous and interesting people come, to live in

◀ The hotel accountant (left) discusses finance with the manager.

elegant surroundings with good food and wine and enjoy plenty of social life. The manager often gives parties for visiting guests and clients and in resort hotels the manager usually gives a welcome cocktail party for new arrivals once a week.

Hotel accountant

There are few accountants in individual hotels. Most are employed by hotel groups and they will tour round hotels looking after their general finances, working out profit and loss, and estimating how much can be advanced and how much money is needed for improvements.

Food and beverage manager

This is a relatively new job, overseeing banqueting, conference and restaurant catering in the hotel. The food and beverage manager is in charge of all aspects of food and drink in the hotel. He has a budget which covers food and drink stores, equipment and machinery, staff and their wages. He works with the chef estimating costs on recipes on a weekly or annual basis and estimates profitability.

In bigger chains, he works to a central manual of recipes and menus. The food and beverage manager oversees purchasing, checks supplies and monitors prices with suppliers. He will check portion control and any wastage in the kitchen, and kitchen experience is very valuable for this management job.

Essential services manager

This is a job found in the larger hotels where someone is needed to coordinate all the items needed by the various departments every day. The essential services manager should have a good knowledge of how other departments work. Essential services are responsible for ensuring that general items, including food, have been ordered and checked in. Checks are kept on the quality of goods with suppliers.

Apart from foodstuffs, the essential services manager controls the stocking of the wine cellar and keeps records of supplies of linen and uniforms. It is also a matter for the essential services manager to discuss any design change in goods which are being replaced.

Experience and a good head for figures are necessary. The job also requires organizational ability and level-headedness, since this department is always under pressure.

▲ A public relations officer arranges a photographic session for a new brochure which the hotel is putting out.

Works manager

The title varies, but this person usually has engineering, architectural or surveying background and is in charge of making sure the hotel machinery works and the structure is kept repaired and decorated.

Under him work plumbers, carpenters, electricians, fitters, and craft workmen who do everything from unblocking a drain to erecting a stage for a conference presentation. Fuel must be used at the most economical rate. The boilers, the heart of the hotel, are carefully maintained: a hotel without hot bath water is a source of many complaints as is erratic air conditioning.

The works manager sees that emergency generators are looked after, that fire-fighting equipment and internal communications systems are kept up to standard and that rooms are painted and redecorated as needed. The works manager is also involved in seeing that new materials are tested, and that carpet and furnishing fabrics are flame-proof.

Often he is involved at design stage in approving furniture design. Hotels sometimes have designs tested by furniture research laboratories for strength and durability. Hotel furniture has to withstand hefty wear and tear and is often made much thicker and sturdier than domestic designs.

Locks and replacement of keys come under this department's work. In hotels with a swimming pool, filtration and heating apparatus would be the concern of the works manager.

Publicity manager

These managers look after the public image and presentation of the hotel and make sure the hotel is known to the general public. In their department, or based in the head office of a group, is the public relations manager. He or she must give interviews to the press, arrange film and fashion shooting backgrounds, often help to produce a hotel magazine and in general handle any publicity stories about the hotel.

Front of house manager

The front of house manager looks after hall porters, reception staff, cashiers, switchboard staff, uniformed staff and overseas advance bookings. He must try to ensure that rooms are not overbooked so that guests do not have to be taken to other hotels at his hotel's expense. If business is slack, he must decide how many discount rates to give to try to encourage more visitors.

Reference section

General Information

In Britain, the catering industry is the fourth largest employer and is still growing along with the big increase in tourism. It's a good idea to get the feel of hotel life. Ask your parents to take you to a meal at a local hotel and stand in the lobby and watch the busy scene. Some hotel groups, like Trust Houses Forte, encourage potential recruits to visit their hotels and will make arrangements for you to see a local one.

Your careers adviser at school will be able to give you general information on the variety of jobs offered and the training courses open to you. The Employment Service Agency has set up a network of special employment offices and staff dealing with the hotel and catering industry. Further information can be obtained from:

The Job Centre
3 Denmark Street
Charing Cross Road
London WC2 8LR

There are Job Centres in most leading cities and initial application can be made at any Jobcentre or Employment Service Agency in Britain. You may also ask for information on careers and courses from the following organizations:

The Careers Information Service of the Hotel and Catering Industry Training Board
PO Box 18
Ramsey House
Central Square
Wembley HA9 7AP

The HCITB produces several guidance booklets providing general introductory information.

The British Hotels, Restaurants and Caterers Association. This is a trade association for proprietors in hotels and catering and gives advice on all careers. The Association also handles student exchanges with hotels abroad. The address is:

The British Hotels, Restaurants and Caterers Association
13 Cork Street
London W1A 2AF

The Hotel Catering and Institutional Management Association
191 Trinity Road
London SW17 7HN

gives information on courses leading to professional qualifications and also provides lists of colleges. It offers a booklet *How to advance your profession* explaining its work and the benefits of membership.

The industry trade papers *Caterer and Hotel Keeper* and *Catering Times* both issue annual magazines detailing the opportunities for jobs in the industry and give lists of colleges and courses as well as hotel group addresses.

Hotel training schemes

Many of the larger groups of hotels have their own training schemes or day or block release study possibilities. Booklets and information can be obtained from the following addresses:

Trust Houses Forte
Group Personnel Department
1 Jermyn Street
London SW1Y 4UH

Hilton International Hotels Ltd
Personnel Office
London Hilton
Park Lane
London W1A 2HH

They have a printed recruitment brochure for chefs, otherwise send individual job descriptions.

Cunard Hotels Limited
Group Training Department
1 Shortlands
Hammersmith
London W6 8DR

Embassy Hotels Ltd
The Training Manager
Allied Breweries (UK) Ltd
Station Street
Burton on Trent
Staffs DE14 1BZ

Management

Management in the hotel industry needs a variety of talents from accountancy to the supervising of people of many nationalities.

School leavers can take a degree or diploma course at a university or college. If you are already in the industry, some hotels have courses leading to membership of the Hotel Catering and Institutional Management Association. For the latter you will need a miniumum of four GCE 'O' level passes or the equivalent.

To begin an HND course in Hotel Catering and Institutional Management, a minimum of five GCE passes including one 'A' level is needed (in Scotland, five SCE including two highers). To apply for a degree course, a minimum of five GCE passes including two 'A' levels (Scotland five SCE including three highers) is required.

The recommended list of 'O' and 'A' level subjects for management studies is: English language, English literature (a subject which tests the applicant's command of English must be included), mathematics, economics, history, geography, sociology, modern languages, a classical language and up to two science subjects.

An OND qualification in the following subjects is accepted for entry to an HND course: hotel and catering operations, institutional housekeeping and catering, hotel catering and institutional operations or business studies.

Two leaflets from the HCIMA explain the qualifications needed as well as entry application and procedure. They also list the colleges at which OND and HND courses in hotel management are run. Degree courses in hotel catering management are available at the following universities:

University of Surrey
Department of Hotel and Catering Management
Guildford
Surrey
GU2 5XH

and

University of Strathclyde
(Scottish Hotel School)
Ross Hall
Crookston Road
Glasgow G5 3NQ

Degree courses are also available at
Huddersfield Polytechnic
Sheffield Polytechnic
Polytechnic of North London
Oxford Polytechnic
Hollings College Manchester
The Hotel Catering and Institutional Management Association

Other colleges particularly associated with courses at varying levels in the hotel and catering industry include:
Bournemouth and Poole College
Department of Catering, Tourism and Hotel Operations
Lansdowne
Bournemouth BH1 3JJ

Ealing College of Higher Education
School of Hotel Keeping and Catering
St Mary's Road
Ealing
London W5 5RF
and
The Westminster College Hotel School
Vincent Square
London SW1P 2PD

Catering
School leavers need a good general education. 'O' levels, CSE passes or the equivalent are an advantage but not essential.

Career courses offer day release study for the following City and Guilds Courses:
706/1 Basic Cooking for the Catering Industry
706/2 Cookery for the Catering Industry
On a day release course, trainees take 706/1 at the end of the second year; 706/2 at the end of the fourth year. With block release, 706/1 is taken after one year and 706/2 at the end of the second year. Once course 706/2 has been passed and experience in the industry gained, City and Guilds 706/3 can be studied on Advanced Cookery.

There is also 705, a general full-time catering course for one year offered to school leavers by a large number of colleges. The course gives a good general basic introduction to the hotel and catering industry.

Food Service
Waiters and Waitresses need a good general education but no specific qualifications. Students should be able to read, write legibly add simple figures and have a reasonable command of English. A pleasant personality, good health, and ability to work under pressure are the main abilities needed. There are schemes for on-the-job training, with release to take City and Guilds Course 707/1, a certificate in food service for waiters and waitresses. Course 707/2 is a course on advanced serving techniques which indicates the ability to be a head waiter or waitress. This can be taken after 707/1 or 705, the general catering course, has been taken. Information on the City and Guilds courses can be obtained (send 30p to include cost and postage) from:
City and Guilds London Institute
76 Portland Place
London W1N 4AA

Licensed Trade Staff
Bar Managers, Wine Waiters and Cooks working in hotels, inns or pubs require a good education and can take courses given by the Licensed Trade Training and Education Committee, sponsored by the Hotel and Catering Industry Training Board. The minimum age of acceptance is 18 years. Information can be obtained from:

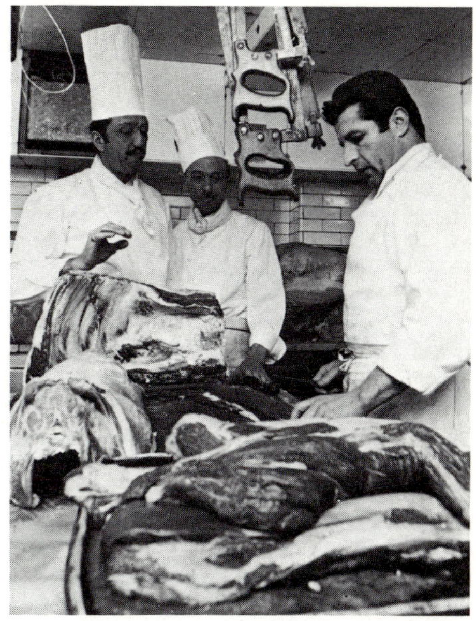

The Retail Trading Department
The Brewers Society
42 Portman Square
London WLH 0BB

Kitchen Staff
Kitchen Porters, Platemen, Service Assistants require no previous experience or educational qualifications and training is done on the job.

Housekeeping Staff
A good education with 'O' levels or CSE equivalent is useful but not essential. The City and Guilds course 708 covering organization, laundry, safety, hygiene, security, interior decorating, and basic staff supervision is required for senior housekeeping jobs and floor housekeepers.

Chambermaids are usually accepted when 18 years old with no qualifications. They may also be students, working during vacations.

Front Office and Reception Staff
The entry qualification is the City and Guilds 709 Hotel Reception course. This is usually a one-year full-time course at a technical college.

A number of hotel groups also offer in-house reception training schemes. The 709 course covers a wide range of subjects including the hotel industry, social skills, salesmanship, legal requirements, reception and its routines, business practice, calculations, book keeping, safety and fire precautions and ancillary duties.

Receptionists and Cashiers need a good, general education. Proficiency in English and arithmetic is essential and a second language is a definite help. A smart appearance and pleasant welcoming personality are other needs to become a good receptionist. Cashiers need 'O' level maths and in some cases one year's experience in hotel work.

Telephonists require Post Office training in the use of their switchboards together with a second language in the bigger international and city hotels.

In Scotland, the hotel reception courses are administered by:
The Scottish Business Education Council
22 Great King Street
Edinburgh EH3 6QH

The Hotel Catering Industry Training Board issues a list of all the colleges in Britain which offer the City and Guilds 709 Hotel Reception Certificate.

Hotel Office Staff
A good general education is required. Other languages are an advantage and a good clear telephone manner is needed.

Advance Reservation Clerks will have to master working with a booking computer or international instant confirmation computer such as the one owned by Holiday Inns, a system called *Holidex*.

Trainee porters are accepted at the age of 18 years and a good education is usually required. The applicant needs to be smart in appearance and have a pleasant manner, for he will be dealing with clients all the time. He must also be fit and able to handle heavy luggage. Speaking a second language is also an advantage for a porter.

Training to be a hall or luggage porter is done on the job and on leaving school larger hotels would take trainees for $1\frac{1}{2}$–$2\frac{1}{2}$ years as junior hall porter or page boy learning to be hall porter or enquiry clerk.

In this time, college release could be obtained to take the City and Guilds Course 710, the Hotel and Uniformed staff certificate.

General Staff
Maintenance staff such as electricians, fitters, plumbers and carpenters, will be expected to have had previous experience and training in their special craft.

Useful Words

Some special terms that are useful to know when working in a hotel.

A la carte menu from which diner selects what he wants; each dish is costed separately. Restaurants also offer *table d'hôte* menu, in which all the courses are served at an inclusive price.

Apartotel building like a hotel with central services, but each room is more like an apartment with cooking facilities.

Bain Marie 'hot bath' used in cooking dishes slowly. Dishes are cooked in a container in a pan of hot water.

Bed nights how a hotel calculates its success – the number of people times the number of nights slept in the hotel.

Bell boy assistant to bell captain.

Bell captain American term for hall porter.

Booking out a term for overbooking a room and having to turn a guest away to another hotel.

Breakfast keys card order forms on which to order breakfast. These are hung on the door knob outside the room by guests.

Check out when the guest leaves and pays his bill.

Coffee shop restaurant open long hours, serving light snack-style or bacon and eggs style of meals.

Crib or cot small bed added to room for a baby or toddler to sleep in.

Dassing a term for letting a double room as a single when occupancy is low.

European plan accommodation is on room only basis with no food included.

Floor waiter waiter who takes things to rooms on a certain floor.

Full American plan full board.

Grill Room usually hotel's smart restaurant.

Italian bed where double bed ordered and only twins are available; the two beds are made into one by putting together and using double-sized sheets and blankets.

Lamp work cooking in restaurant done by head waiter over a small lamp, using methylated spirits as fuel, usually items like *steak diane* or *crêpes suzette*.

Lobby entrance area of a hotel.

Mezzanine split-level floor between ground and first floor. Usually has balcony overlooking lobby.

Modified American plan half-board. Food is included in accommodation terms.

Motel hotel especially for motorists with adjacent parking space.

No show guests booked do not turn up.

Penthouse luxury suite at top of hotel.

Rollaway moveable bed which can be put in a room on request.

Room service directory list of facilities and services offered by hotel and detailed in booklet in bedroom.

Salamander grill with heat coming from above; the grill in a hotel kitchen is usually charcoal with heat from below.

Section number of rooms allocated to a maid to clean. Can be on different floor levels.

Short order a light food dish or snack.

Slept out guest is booked into his room and belongings are there, but he has not slept in his room.

Star system the way many countries grade hotels. Five star is de luxe rating.

Suite series of rooms including sitting room with bedroom and bathroom.

VIP Very Important Person. Someone the hotel wants to look after especially and who receives special treatment. Items such as fruit and flowers are put in room.

Books

A Hotel and Catering Career by John Fuller, Barrie and Jenkins 1976
Catering (People at Work Series) by Charles King, Blackie 1976
Choosing a Job in a Hotel by Hugh Thompson, Wayland 1976
Careers in Catering by Littlewood, Pitman 1971

Films

The HCITB have produced two colour films:
People Who Like People and *Open to Choice.*
These are available on free loan.
Details from:
Film Library
Central Office of Information
Bromyard Avenue
London W3 7JB

J. Lyons
Cadby Hall
Hammersmith Road
London W14
have the following films available:
Hygiene, the Key to Cleanliness
Hygiene for Food and Restaurant Staff (slides and tape) and
The Uninvited Guest (fire prevention)

Acknowledgements

Key to the position of illustrations: (T) top; (C) centre; (B) bottom; and combinations, for example: (TR) top right, or (CL) centre left.

Artists
John Fraser: 19, 20–21
John Shackell: 11, 25, 26, 28–29, 30, 33
Barrie Thorpe/David Lewis Management: 12–13, 14, 31, 34
Bob Harvey/David Lewis Management: 22, 40–41
Roland Berry: 4, 20, 26
Shoestring: 18
Mike Whittlesea/Temple Art: 6–7

Photographs
Featurepix: front cover
Spectrum: back cover, 5(BR), 37(BL,TR)
Churchill Hotel: 9(TL), 29(BR), 45(BL)
De Vere Hotels and Restaurants Ltd: 9(TR)
Illustrated London News: 10, 23(TR), 33
Wells O'Brien: 15(TR), 36(BL)
Athenaeum Hotel: 19
John Topham: 24
Bill Holden: 27(BR)
Trust Houses Forte: 29(TR), 35(BR)
Rank Hotels: 34
British Tourist Authority: 36(BR), 37(BR)
Holiday Inns: 37(TL)
Savoy Hotel: 45(TR)
Geg Germany: 9(BL,BR), 11, 14, 15(B), 16, 17(TR), 18 21 (TR,B), 22, 23(TL,BR), 25, 27(T), 28, 30, 31, 32, 35(TL,BL, TR), 38, 39(TL,TR,B), 42(BL,TR), 43, 46

Information
The Author and Publishers would like to thank all the staff of the Tower Hotel, London, for their helpful cooperation in photography and in providing information; in particular, Linda Abrahams, the publicity officer and executive chef Bob Hughes. The Author would also like to thank the manager and staff of the Cavendish Hotel, London, for similar help in providing pictures and information, also Holiday Inn staff, Swiss Cottage, Trust Houses Forte personnel department and Christopher Bond, Chief Executive, Embassy Hotels.

Index

Numbers in *italics* refer to illustrations